EXPERIMENTS WITH ELECTRICITY

A TRUE BOOK

by
Salvatore Tocci

Children's Press®
A Division of Scholastic Inc.

New York Toronto London Auckland Sydney
Mexico City New Delhi Hong Kong
Danbury, Connecticut

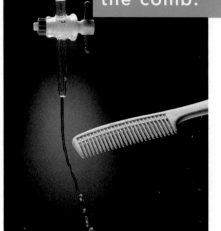

The water bends because of static electricity from the comb.

Reading Consultant
Jeanne Clidas, *Rigby Education*
Danbury, CT

Nanci Vargus, *Primary Multiage Teacher*
Decatur Township Schools
Indianapolis, Indiana

Science Consultants
Robert Gardner, *Salisbury Schools,*
Salisbury, CT

Kevin Beardmore, *Indiana Dept. of Ed.*

Richard Anderson, *Westhampton Beach*
Elementary School, Westhampton Beach, NY

The author and publisher are not responsible for injuries or accidents that occur during or from any experiments. Experiments should be conducted in the presence of or with the help of an adult. Any instructions of the experiments that require the use of sharp, hot, or other unsafe items should be conducted by or with the help of an adult.

Library of Congress Cataloging-in-Publication Data

Tocci, Salvatore.
    Experiments with electricity / by Salvatore Tocci.
        p. cm. — (A true book)
    Includes bibliographical references and index.
    ISBN 0-516-22247-3 (lib. bdg.)   0-516-27348-5 (pbk.)
    1. Electricity—Experiments—Juvenile literature. [1. Electricity—
Experiments. 2. Experiments.] I. Title II. Series.

QC527.2.T63 2001
537'.078—dc21   00-065596

Contents

Touching a door knob can make a small spark.

Why Do Sparks Fly?

Did you ever get a small shock from touching a doorknob? This shock comes from a tiny spark that flies from your hand to the doorknob. This spark is so small that you probably don't see it.

There is a huge spark that you can sometimes see on a

During a thunderstorm, huge sparks zoom from the clouds to the earth.

rainy day. Lightning is a group of huge sparks that fly from a cloud to the ground during a rain storm. As the lightning zooms through the air, it makes a huge noise called thunder.

Why does a spark fly from your hand to a doorknob or from a cloud to the ground? Why is a spark of lightning so much bigger? You can learn the answers to these questions by doing experiments with something you use every day—electricity.

What Is Electricity?

To understand what electricity is, you first need to learn about something that is too small to see: an atom. Everything on Earth, including you, is made of atoms. Each atom is made of smaller bits called particles. These particles are electrons, protons, and neutrons. The

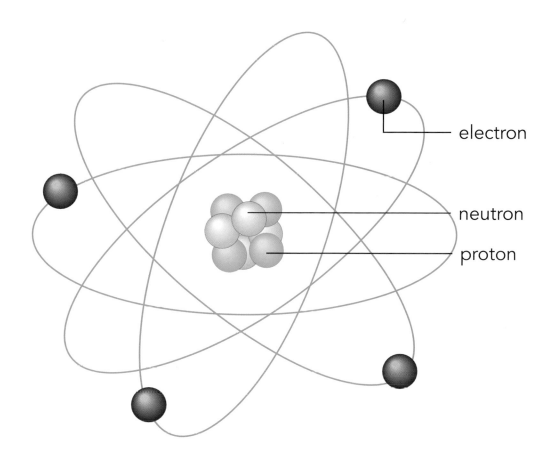

electron

neutron

proton

Electrons move very quickly around the center of the atom.

electrons zoom around the center of an atom where the protons and neutrons are.

An atom contains two types of charges—positive (+) and negative (–). The protons in the center of an atom have a positive charge, and the electrons have a negative charge. An atom usually has the same number of protons (positive charges) and electrons (negative charges). Because of this equal number, the atom itself has no charge.

However, atoms can develop charges. So how does that happen?

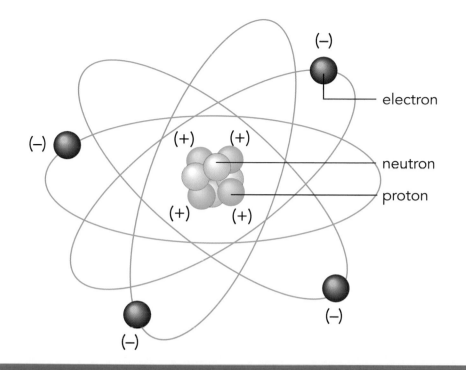

(−)

electron

(−)

(+)   (+)

neutron

proton

(+)   (+)

(−)

(−)

How many negative charges does this atom have? How many positive charges does it have? The negative charges cancel the positive charges, so the atom has no charge.

Electrons can move from one atom to another. When electrons move, the atom develops a charge. If an atom gains an

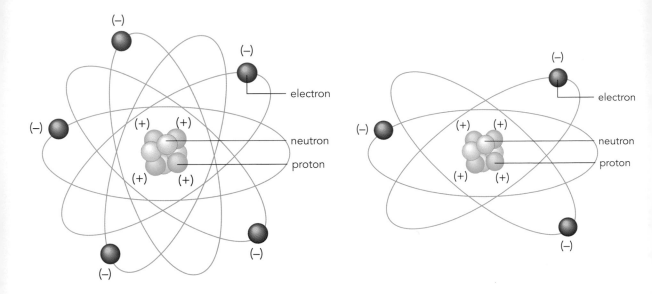

electron, it develops a negative charge. If an atom gives up an electron, it develops a positive charge.

For example, count the number of electrons in the atom shown on the left. Next count the number of protons in its center. You should have five electrons and four protons. Because it has one more electron than proton, it has a negative charge. Now count the number of electrons in the atom shown on the right. Next count the number of protons in its center. You should have three electrons and four protons. Because it has one more proton than electron, it has a positive charge.

How can you make electrons move from one atom to another?

Making Electrons Move

You will need:
- two balloons
- string
- a wool sock

Blow up two balloons with air. Tie a short piece of string to each balloon. Rub both balloons with a wool sock. Hold the two balloons by the string and bring them together. What happens?

Rub just one balloon again with the sock. Then bring the balloon near the sock. What happens?

The two balloons are rubbed with the sock and brought together.

Next, turn on a faucet. The water must flow in a steady, narrow stream. What happens when you hold the same balloon near the water?

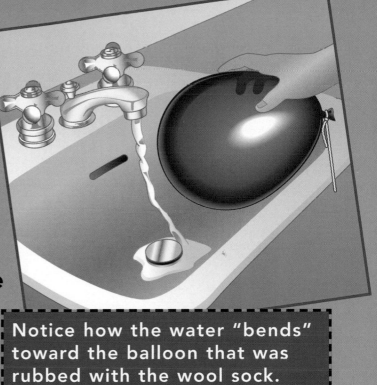

Notice how the water "bends" toward the balloon that was rubbed with the wool sock.

The atoms that make up wool give up their electrons very easily. When you rubbed the two balloons with the sock, you caused electrons to move from the sock to the balloons.

Both balloons rubbed with the sock moved away from each other because they have the same charge.

By gaining electrons, both balloons developed negative charges. Objects that have the same charge move away from each other. Because the two balloons had the same charge, they moved away from each other.

As for the wool sock, it lost electrons when you rubbed the balloon with it. So it developed a positive charge. Objects that have different charges move toward each other. The sock and the balloon had different charges, so they moved closer to each other. Can you explain why

The balloon is covered with negative charges. The sock has positive charges. Different charges attract each other.

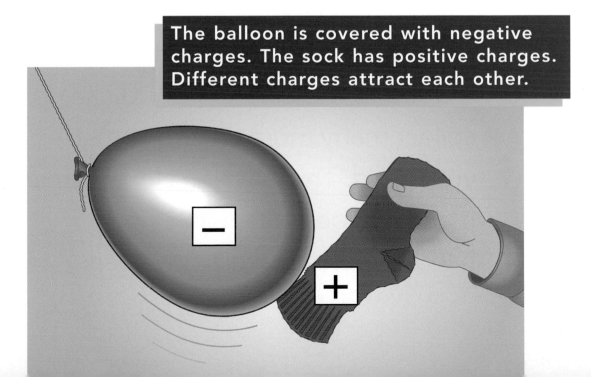

the water and the balloon moved closer to each other?

Sometimes electrons will jump from an object with a negative charge to an object with a positive charge. When this happens, a spark is made. A tiny spark occurs when electrons jump from your hand to a doorknob. Huge sparks, or lightning, occur when electrons fly down from a cloud to the earth. A cloud can collect many more electrons than your hand. This is why a cloud can make a huge spark, while your hand can only make a tiny spark.

Some of the clothes are covered with positive charges. Other clothes are covered with negative charges. Because of static electricity, the clothes cling together.

Whether they are small or huge, sparks are caused by static electricity. You can get static electricity when two objects with different charges come together. For example, static electricity sometimes causes clothes to cling together. What else can static electricity do?

Using Static Electricity

You will need:
- a small fluorescent lightbulb
- a plastic comb
- a wool sock

Take these objects into a dark closet. Rub the comb with the sock for at least a minute. Touch the comb to the middle of the lightbulb. What do you see? Look closely inside the bulb.

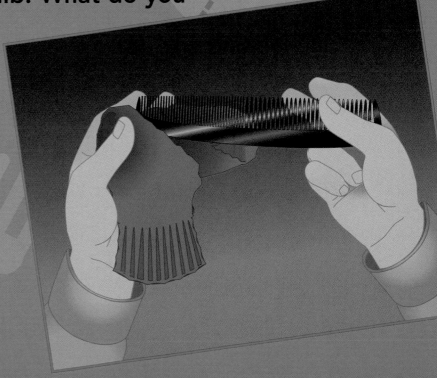

The electrons coming from the comb light the bulb.

Electrons jumped from the comb to the bulb and made small sparks inside the bulb. Static electricity caused the bulb to light for just a short time. To get it to stay lit, electrons must keep flowing through the bulb. This steady flow of electrons produces current electricity, or what we simply call electricity.

How Does Electricity Flow?

Electricity usually flows in a loop. This loop is called an electric circuit. In an electric circuit, electrons flow through a complete path and return to their starting point. For example, think of an electric circuit as a running track. The runners

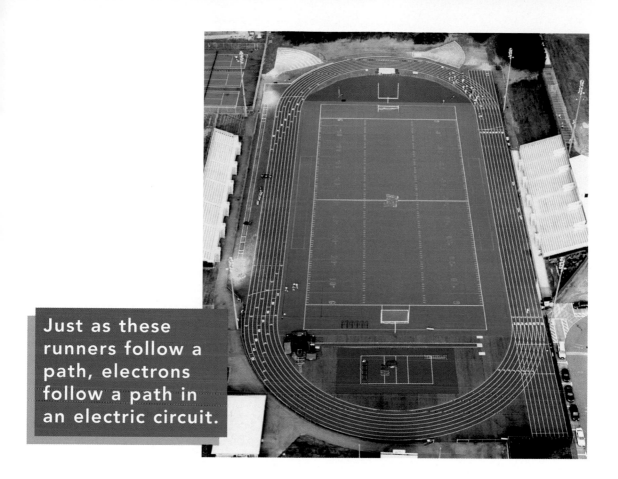

Just as these runners follow a path, electrons follow a path in an electric circuit.

race around the track or loop over and over again. Is there a way to tell if electrons are flowing through a circuit over and over again?

Experiment 3

Building an Electric Circuit

You will need:
- a flashlight
- electrical tape
- bare copper wire
- scissors

Remove the two batteries and bulb from the flashlight. Use electrical tape to join together the two batteries just as they are in the flashlight. You will then need to cut two short pieces of copper wire. Tape one end of one piece of wire to the bottom end of the batteries. Tape one end of the other piece of wire to the top end of the batteries.

Touch the free ends of both wires to the bulb as shown in the photos. What happens to the bulb?

Be sure to touch one wire to the base of the bulb and the other to the metal piece around the side of the bulb.

The electrons started flowing from the bottom of the battery through the copper wire. Then they flowed into the bulb and made it light up! The electrons then flowed from the bulb through the other copper wire that is connected to the top of the battery. The electrons traveled in a loop, or through a complete circuit.

Copper wire allows electrons to flow freely. Anything that allows electrons to flow is

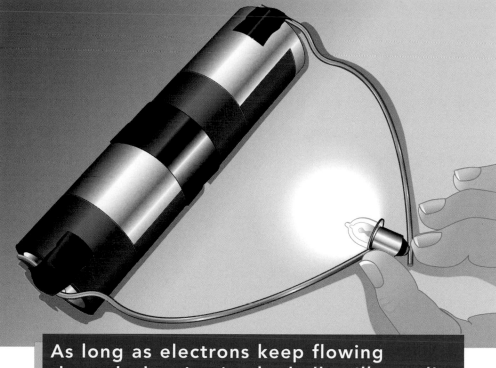

As long as electrons keep flowing through the circuit, the bulb will stay lit.

called a conductor. Some things do not allow electrons to flow, and they are called insulators. How can you find out whether something is a conductor or an insulator?

Identifying Conductors and Insulators

You will need:
- bulb with threaded base
- bulb holder
- scissors
- ruler
- bare copper wire
- screw driver
- electrical tape
- string
- coin
- rubber band
- paper clip

Screw the bulb into the bulb holder. Connect two 6-inch pieces of wire to the bulb holder. Tape one wire to the bottom of one of the batteries. Tape the other wire to the top of the battery. The bulb should light up.

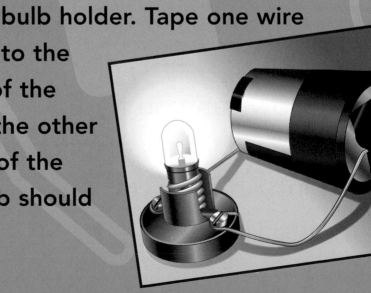

> If the paper clip allows electrons to flow, the bulb will light up.

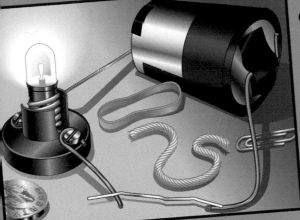

Cut one of the wires. What happens? Straighten a paper clip. Use it to touch both ends of the cut wire. What happens? Do the same with the piece of string, coin, and rubber band. Which of these are conductors? Which are insulators? Test other objects you have at home to see if they are conductors or insulators.

There are times when you may want to "turn off" and then "turn on" the flow of electrons. For example, a light switch in your home works this way. How does a light switch work?

Building a Switch

You will need:
- bulb holder
- scissors
- ruler
- bare copper wire
- screw driver
- electrical tape
- pliers
- two thumbtacks
- metal paper clip
- small piece of wood

Follow the instructions in Experiment 4 to set up an electrical circuit. However, this time screw two 10-inch pieces of wire to the bulb holder. Be sure that the bulb lights up.

Cut one of the wires. Use pliers to make a small loop at each end of the cut wire. Insert a thumbtack through one loop. Then, push the thumbtack and looped wire into the wood.

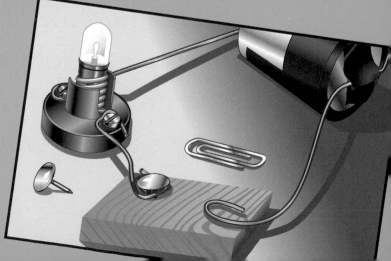

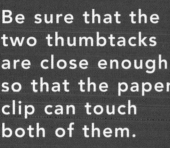

Insert another thumbtack through a paper clip. Then push the thumbtack and paper clip through the other loop of the cut wire and into the wood.

Swing the paper clip so that it touches both thumbtacks. The paper clip acts as a switch. The switch allows electricity to flow through the circuit to light the bulb. The switch is on when the paper clip touches both thumbtacks.

Be sure that the two thumbtacks are close enough so that the paper clip can touch both of them.

When the paper clip touches both thumbtacks, the switch is on.

Swing the paper clip away from the thumbtack. The switch is now off, and electricity cannot flow through the circuit to light the bulb.

A switch often turns on and off more than one light. How does this work? This is done by connecting the lights in either a series circuit or in a parallel circuit. How is a series circuit different from a parallel circuit?

Building Series and Parallel Circuits

You will need:
- two flashlights
- electrical tape
- two bulb holders
- bare copper wire
- ruler
- scissors
- pliers

Take apart the two flashlights. Tape the two batteries together just as they are in the flashlight. Unscrew the bulbs. Then screw each one into the bulb holder. Connect the two bulb holders with a 6-inch piece of wire. Cut two 12-inch pieces of wire. Connect the end of one 12-inch wire to one bulb holder. Then tape the other end of this wire to the top

of the batteries. Connect the second 12 inch wire from the bottom of the batteries to the other bulb holder. You now have a series circuit. Both bulbs should be lit.

Now unscrew one of the bulbs. What happened to the lights? They both should go out. Screw the bulb back in. Now unscrew the other bulb. Did both lights go out again? Unscrewing either bulb breaks the circuit. Electricity can no longer flow through the circuit. Without electricity, both bulbs go out.

Unscrew all the wires from the bulb holders. Keep the 12-inch wires taped to the batteries. Screw the free ends of the two 12-inch wires into one

These bulbs are connected in a parallel circuit. With your finger, trace the path that electrons follow to light each bulb.

of the bulb hold-ers. Cut another 6-inch piece of wire. Screw the two 6-inch wires into the second bulb holder. Then use pliers to twist the free end of one of the 6-inch wires around the 12-inch wire. Twist the free end of the 6-inch wire around the other 12-inch wire. You now have a parallel circuit.

What happens when you unscrew either one of the bulbs that are connected in a parallel circuit? Unscrewing one bulb does not cause the other bulb to go out. This is because electricity can still flow through a circuit to light the bulb.

What Else Can Electricity Do?

Electricity powers your television at home and your computer at school. It can heat many homes and can make the sounds you hear on the television or radio.

You probably were aware that electricity can provide light, heat, and sound. However, you

You may have seen a magnet like this at school.

probably did not know that electricity can also turn something into a magnet. A magnet is anything that attracts or sticks to iron or steel. You have seen small magnets hold pictures and papers on refrigerators. How can you use electricity to make a magnet?

Making a Magnet

You will need:
- large steel nail
- flashlight battery
- plastic insulated copper wire with ends stripped
- thumbtacks
- scissors or wire stripper

Wrap the insulated copper wire around the length of a steel nail. Hold the wire at an insulated part and touch the bare ends of the wire to a flashlight battery for several seconds. What happens when you bring the nail near some thumbtacks?

The nail has become an electromagnet.

Stereo speakers, televisions, and computer monitors need electromagnets to work.

An electric current caused the nail to become an electromagnet. An electromagnet is an object that becomes a magnet because of electricity. There are a number of items in your home that need electromagnets to work.

You have learned that electrons flowing through a circuit supply electricity. You can stop the flow of electrons by using an insulator or by throwing a switch. Sometimes, electrons jump from one place to another. When this happens, you may get a tiny shock when you touch a door knob, or see large sparks of lightning.

Fun With Electricity

Now that you've learned about electricity, here's a fun experiment to do. You can make tiny sparks fly any time you want. You won't even have to touch anything.

Making Sparks

You will need:
- scissors
- masking tape
- Polystyrene foam tray (used to package meats in the supermarket)
- table
- aluminum pie tin

First thing you want to do is cut an L-shaped piece from the polystyrene tray. Tape this piece to the center of the pie tin. Quickly rub the bottom of the rest of the tray through your hair. Electrons will jump from your hair to the tray. Place the tray down on a table and darken the room. Use the L-shaped piece to pick up the pie tin. Hold the tin about one foot from the tray. Drop it so that it falls on the tray. Slowly bring your finger toward the pie tin.

Do you see a tiny spark? This spark was made from electrons that jumped from the tray to the tin and then to your hand. Now use the L-shaped piece to pick up the pie tin. Slowly bring your finger to it. Did you get another spark? This time electrons jumped from your finger back to the pie tin. Again, drop the pie tin onto the tray. You should get another spark. You can keep getting sparks by doing this over and over. When you don't get any more sparks, just rub the tray through your hair and start over.

Use the polystyrene foam piece as a handle whenever you have to lift the pie tin.

To Find Out More

If you would like to learn more about electricity, check out these additional resources.

 **Books**

Bartholomew, Alan. **Electric Gadgets and Gizmos: Battery-Powered Buildable Gadgets That Go!** Kids Can Press, 1998.

Cole, Joanna. **The Magic School Bus and the Electric Field Trip.** Scholastic Inc., 1999.

dePinna, Simon. **Electricity.** Raintree Steck-Vaughn, 1998.

Nankivell-Aston, Sally and Dorothy Jackson. **Science Experiments With Electricity.** Franklin Watts, 2000.

Organizations and Online Sites

The Baken
3537 Zenith Avenue South
Minneapolis, MN
55416-4623
612-927-6508
http://www.baken museum.org/

This learning center deals only with electricity and magnetism. You can visit an image gallery and contact them for publications, programs, and kits that deal with electricity.

The Franklin Institute Science Museum
22 North 20th Street
Philadelphia, PA 19103
215-448-1200
http://sln.fi.edu/tfi/ welcome.html

This organization has information on Benjamin Franklin's famous experiments with electricity. Find out what Franklin learned about electricity when he flew a kite during a thunderstorm.

The Exploratorium
3601 Lyon Street
San Francisco, CA 94123
http://www.exploratorium. edu/

Their site has many simple experiments that you can do to learn more about electricity. You can even start your own electric flea circus. You can find out how to make your own very, very tiny lightning anytime you want by logging on to *http://www. exploratorium.edu/ science_explorer/sparker. html*

Important Words

atom tiny particle that makes up you or anything else

conductor something that allows electricity to flow

current electricity made when electrons flow

electric circuit path that electrons follow

electromagnet a magnet made by using electricity

electron part of an atom that has a negative charge

insulator something that does not allow electricity to flow

parallel circuit where electricity can flow along more than one path

series circuit where electricity can flow along only one path

static electricity made when electrons jump between two objects

Index

Meet the Author

Salvatore Tocci is a science writer who lives in East Hampton, New York, with his wife, Patti. He was a high school biology and chemistry teacher for almost 30 years. As a teacher, he always encouraged his students to do experiments to learn about science. When he is not writing, he is busy using electricity to build and run his large HO-model train layout.

Photographs ©: Peter Arnold Inc./Keith Kent: 1; Photo Researchers, NY: 6 (Keith Kent/SPL), 2 (Charles D. Winters); Photodisc, Inc.: cover, 23, 39; PhotoEdit/Tony Freeman/MR: 37; Visuals Unlimited/Jeff J. Daly: 4.

Illustrations by Patricia Rasch